Let's Explore Antarctica!

by Colin Kong

PEARSON

Scott
Foresman

Editorial Offices: Glenview, Illinois • Parsippany, New Jersey • New York, New York
Sales Offices: Needham, Massachusetts • Duluth, Georgia • Glenview, Illinois
Coppell, Texas • Ontario, California • Mesa, Arizona

Photographs

Every effort has been made to secure permission and provide appropriate credit for photographic material. The publisher deeply regrets any omission and pledges to correct errors called to its attention in subsequent editions.

Unless otherwise acknowledged, all photographs are the property of Pearson Education, Inc.

Photo locators denoted as follows: Top (T), Center (C), Bottom (B), Left (L), Right (R), Background (Bkgd)

Cover ©Volodymyr Goinyk/Shutterstock; 1 Jurgen Ziewe/Ikon Images/Alamy Images; 3 Commander John Bortniak/NOAA; 6 ©Royalty-Free/Corbis; 7 Eric Carr/Alamy Images; 8 Michael Van Woert/NOAA; 9 Jurgen Ziewe/Ikon Images/Alamy Images; 10 ©Volodymyr Goinyk/Shutterstock; 11 (T) Chaikovskiy Igor/Shutterstock, (BC) Michael Van Woert/NOAA, (BR) Thinkstock, (TC) Tom Brakefield/Thinkstock; 12 (B) Hemera/Thinkstock; 13 INTERFOTO/Alamy Images; 14 Volodymyr Goinyk/Shutterstock; 15 (T) blickwinkel/Alamy Images, (CL) NASA; 17 Fritz Poelking/Picture Press/Alamy Images; 18 blickwinkel/Alamy Images; 19 Robert Harding Picture Library Ltd/Alamy Images; 20 NGS Collection/Alamy; 21 imagebroker/Alamy; 22 (CR) ©Royalty-Free/Corbis, (B) imagebroker/Alamy, (TL) NGS Collection/Alamy.

ISBN: 0-328-13482-1

14 15 16 17 V0FL 16 15 14 13

Antarctica is a **continent** located at the southern pole of our planet. In fact, Antarctica is one of the polar ice caps. The other polar ice cap is at the northern pole of the planet.

If you are planning to **depart** for Antarctica, be sure to pack plenty of warm clothing. It is a land of extremes. Fierce winds and blinding storms are common there. In fact, Antarctica is the coldest, highest, windiest, and driest continent on earth!

Nobody really lives in Antarctica. The land is mostly untouched. No country owns Antarctica, either. Instead, different countries have signed an agreement to study Antarctica. Among other things, they study the effects of wind, water, and light on the Antarctic surface.

GEOGRAPHIC SOUTH POLE
AVERAGE TEMP MINUS 56°F
ALTITUDE 9186
ICE THICKNESS OVER 9000

Antarctica: Land of Extremes

Coldest	World low temperature record of -129° F (-89.4° C) at Vostok on July 21, 1983
Highest	Average elevation of 8200 ft. (2500 m)
Windiest	Gale winds reach 200 mi/hr (320 km/hr) on Commonwealth Bay, George V coast
Driest	Average precipitation is less than 2 in. (5 cm) per year

Antarctica's Chilly Surface

Blizzards and cold temperatures can threaten the scientists who come to study Antarctica. Sometimes they have to stay inside their tents for days at a time because the winds are too strong. They wait with **anticipation** for the terrible weather to stop.

Imagine that you are in the middle of Antarctica. What do you see? Snow, ice, and more ice! More than 99% of the continent is covered in ice—about 5.3 million square miles (13.7 million square kilometers). The Antarctic Ice Sheet is millions of years old and up to three miles deep.

Why is Antarctica so important? For starters, around 90% of the fresh water on the Earth's surface is found in this Ice Sheet. Also, about 90% of the world's ice is found on this continent. All oceans around the world contain water that came from the ice of Antarctica. If the Antarctic Ice Sheet were to melt, the ocean's waters would rise by 196 to 213 feet (60 to 65 meters). This would create terrible flooding.

ATLANTIC
OCEAN

NORWEGIAN DEPENDENCY

INDIAN
OCEAN

BRITISH TERRITORY

INE CLAIM

a

Average permanent e

The Transantarctic
Mountains separate
West Antarctica
from East Antarctica.

Dronning Maud Land

Enderby Land

Graham
Land
Antarctic
Peninsula

Weddell
Sea

Palmer Land

Ma Robertson Land

AUSTRALIAN ANTARCTIC TERRITORY

Ronne
Ice Shelf

AMERICAN
HIGHLAND

Amery
Ice Shelf

Bellinghausen
Sea

Ellsworth
Land

South Pole

GREATER
ANTARCTICA

Queen Mary
Land

Shackleton
Ice Shelf

Amundsen
Sea

LESSER
ANTARCTICA

Marie Byrd
Land

Mount Erebus is
an active volcano.
It has a permanent
molten lava lake.

Ross Ice
Shelf

Mt. Erebus

oss
Sea

TRANSANTARCTIC MOUNTAINS

Wilkes Land

Victoria Land

Dates Land

George V
Land

South
Magnetic
Pole

FRENCH TERRITORY

CIFIC
EAN

ROSS DEPENDENCY (NEW ZEALAND)

Ice caves in
Victoria Land

5

The Geography of Antarctica

Antarctica consists of two very different geological regions. East Antarctica is a vast area the size of the United States. It is made up of continental crust—the Earth's surface. Here the ice sheet averages 1.6 miles (2.57 kilometers) in thickness. It rarely breaks up because it sits squarely on top of the Earth's surface.

Much of the West Antarctic Ice Sheet is below sea level.

Much of West Antarctica—the smaller part of the continent—is below sea level. In some places it can be as much as 1.5 miles (2.4 kilometers) below sea level. Because of this, the West Antarctic Ice Sheet breaks up more easily than the East Antarctic Ice Sheet. In West Antarctica, enormous floating blocks of ice, or glaciers, are in constant motion. The ice can crack and break. For this reason, the landscape is always changing.

Antarctica also has mountains as high as 16,400 feet (5,000 meters). The Transantarctic Mountains divide the continent in two. Most of this range is buried under ice. Part of this range forms the Antarctic Peninsula, which sticks out into the sea like a tail.

The Desert of Antarctica

Did you know that Antarctica can be called a desert? Not all deserts are hot and dry. A desert is an area that gets less than 10 inches (25.4 centimeters) of precipitation in one year. Antarctica falls into this category.

The inner part of the continent receives two inches of moisture in the form of snow per year. This is less moisture than the Sahara Desert gets. Antarctica's coasts get a little more snow—about eight inches of precipitation per year. Heavy snowfalls occur when storms pick up moisture from the seas.

In most deserts, precipitation evaporates. In Antarctica, the precipitation never evaporates. The snow never goes away. It builds up over hundreds of thousands of years and creates very thick ice sheets. As a result, Antarctica's surface only gets thicker.

In parts of Antarctica, called the Dry Valleys, it has not rained for at least two million years!

Snow crystals accumulate year after year to form dense ice on Antarctica's surface.

The Antarctic Ice Sheet

How thick is the Antarctic Ice Sheet? No one knows for sure. Scientists have measured one deep hole in West Antarctica called the Bentley Subglacial Trench. It is 8,200 feet (2,499 meters) deep. It's covered with more than 9,843 feet (3,000 meters) of ice and snow. In fact, some scientists believe the layer of ice could be up to 16,400 feet (5,000 meters) thick!

How does the ice get so thick? Remember, the temperatures in Antarctica are below 32°F (0°C)—even in the summer. Frost and snow crystals that fall on the ice sheet's surface never melt. They accumulate annually, and the crystals begin to be buried by the weight of the crystals above them. After awhile, the snow crystals get compacted and form dense ice. Antarctica has an average elevation of 7,550 feet (2,300 meters). It is the ice that makes the elevation so high.

Scientists have studied what is beneath icebergs, but the evidence is inconclusive.

The Mystery of Antarctica

With so much ice in Antarctica, there is no telling what is underneath the icy surface. Some scientists think there is volcanic activity under certain areas of the ice. They have found places where glaciers and ice streams flow more quickly.

Scientists think volcanic activity melts the ice. Then the quickly flowing water causes Antarctic glaciers and ice streams to move faster. It is amazing to imagine volcanoes erupting under the surface of the polar ice cap!

Danger! Icebergs!

Antarctica's ice sheets are always changing. Sometimes they crack and break. Along the coasts of Antarctica, when an enormous piece **heaves** into the sea, it becomes a floating mountain of ice.

Icebergs then start drifting and moving around, depending on wind speed, wind direction, surface currents, and the size of the **iceberg.** When the wind and currents move icebergs, they act as if they had minds of their own. Icebergs can present very real and pressing dangers to ships that cross in their paths.

A man standing next to an iceberg looks like a tiny ant.

Definitions of Ice Terms

Ice Domes

Ice domes are slow moving areas of ice and snow on an ice sheet. They are dome shaped, and ice flows from the center of the dome. An ice sheet can have several ice domes.

Ice Streams and Outlet Glaciers

Ice streams and outlet glaciers are the fastest moving areas of an ice sheet. They move ice away from ice domes quickly.

Ice Shelves

An ice shelf is a floating ice mass that is attached to an ice sheet on at least one edge. The Ross Ice Shelf in Antarctica is the largest in the world. It is the size of Texas!

Icebergs

Icebergs are pieces of floating ice that break off from ice shelves, outlet glaciers, or ice streams. There are many shapes and sizes of icebergs. Ice shelves produce the majority of icebergs. They also produce some of the largest icebergs.

The movement of icebergs depends on many factors such as wind speed and surface currents.

Icebergs and Sea Currents on the Move!

Winds blow icebergs all around the coast of the continent. Icebergs usually move slowly, and sometimes get stuck in shallow areas. The larger icebergs travel around the continent and eventually migrate to the Weddell Sea. There, they often get stuck. That is why there are large numbers of icebergs along the east coast of the Antarctic Peninsula.

The number and size of icebergs get smaller as you move away from Antarctica. Waves, storms, and warmer waters slowly break down icebergs as they move away from the southern pole. Slowly icebergs melt into the sea.

An iceberg may look large on the surface, but you are not seeing the whole picture. The part of the iceberg under the water can be almost ten times larger in size!

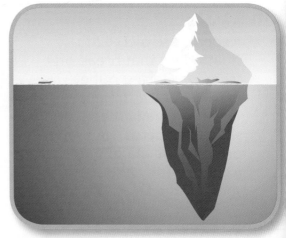

The Tragedy of the Titanic

Did you know that nine-tenths of an iceberg is underwater? Even if you see an iceberg, you can't tell the size of its underwater part. Scientists have found some icebergs that sit deeper than 984 feet (300 meters) under the water. The biggest iceberg discovered was 183 mi (295 km) long and 23 mi (37 km) wide. Its surface area was the size of the Bahamas or the state of Connecticut! Its underwater part was 10 times larger than the part that was visible above water.

All ships try to avoid the path of an iceberg. Icebergs are so hard that they can break rocks. Running into an iceberg is like running directly into a concrete wall. Every crew knows that by the time you see an iceberg up close, it may be too late to avoid crashing into it since its biggest part is underwater.

In 1912, the huge luxury ocean liner *RMS Titanic* hit an iceberg on its first journey across the Atlantic. Within hours, the ship—thought to be unsinkable—broke in two and sank in icy waters. Many passengers were rescued, but many more died.

After running into an iceberg, the *RMS Titanic* ocean liner sank.

Water, Salty Ice, and Light

Water from clouds affects the thickness of Antarctica's surface. Water from the sea has a different effect. The ocean around Antarctica forms sea ice, which is a type of salty ice. In the winter, the area of sea ice formed is about one and a half times the area of the continent. During the other seasons, the sea ice melts to cool both the ocean and the atmosphere. Because the amount of sea ice around its coasts keeps changing, the size of Antarctica grows and shrinks throughout the year.

With such low temperatures all year long, sunlight does not have much of a warming effect on Antarctica's surface. It may be affected by ultraviolet light, however. Ultraviolet (UV) light from the sun is absorbed by the Earth's ozone layer.

The hole in the ozone layer lets more ultraviolet light come through the Earth's atmosphere. The increase in UV rays is harmful to Antarctica's penguins and fish.

Dangers of the Ozone Layer

There is a hole in the ozone layer which poses a big problem for plants and animals in Antarctica. This hole means that more ultraviolet light is entering the Earth's atmosphere. Ultraviolet rays also go into the ocean's waters. As a result, they harm Antarctica's aquatic life, such as fish and marine plants.

It isn't just plants and fish that are in danger. Researchers and scientists in Antarctica also need to be careful to protect themselves from these harmful rays. These rays do not directly affect Antarctica's surface, but they affect life on the surface.

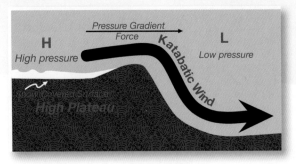

Katabatic winds form when cold winds rush down a steep slope. The strongest katabatic winds are found in Antarctica.

The Effects of Wind

Strong winds are always blowing in Antarctica. Calm periods are rare and usually last only a few hours. At times, it seems as if Antarctica gets more snowfall than it really does. This is because the winds pick up snow from one place and move it to another. The strongest winds are katabatic winds.

The center of the East Antarctic Ice Sheet is called the Polar Plateau. Here, the air is especially cold. The colder the air is, the more dense and heavy it becomes. Because the air is heavy, it settles close to the ground. Due to gravity, the cold and dense air then flows from the interior of the continent toward the coast. Think of a river and you will have an idea of how this cold air flows along Antarctica's surface.

Most winds from the interior of the continent move over gentle slopes. Different grooves in the land cause a **convergence** of air. When air converges, the wind strengthens. Incredibly intense winds, called katabatic winds, pick up speed.

Gravity's Effect on Winds

Gravity also affects the speed of katabatic winds. It can cause wind speeds to suddenly increase from zero to 33.5 to 44.75 miles per hour (15 to 20 meters per second)!

There are two types of katabatic winds. Ordinary katabatic winds flow in one direction, but wind speeds change a lot. Extraordinary katabatic winds can blow for days or weeks at very high speeds.

Katabatic winds can be found in many places around the world. These winds are created when cooled air moves down a steep slope. Antarctica has the strongest katabatic winds on the planet.

Winds are constantly blowing on the continent. The windiest spot on Earth is Cape Denison in Antarctica. Wind speeds here have reached up to 200 miles per hour (320 kilometers per hour).

Antarctica's Cape Denison is sometimes called the Home of the Blizzard.

Danger! Katabatic Winds and Blizzards!

Katabatic winds are most active in winter. They can reach high speeds as they come close to the coast. Katabatic winds have slower speeds at the center of the continent. The windiest spot on Earth is Cape Denison in Antarctica. This is where katabatic winds converge. Sometimes wind speeds reach up to 200 miles per hour (320 kilometers per hour).

It is not easy for researchers to study katabatic winds. Not only are they very strong, but they also carry ice crystals.

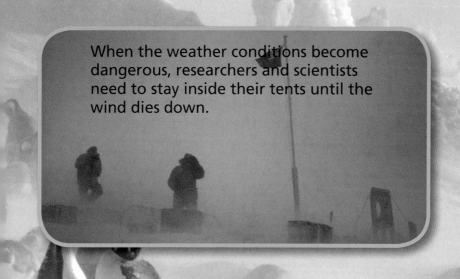

When the weather conditions become dangerous, researchers and scientists need to stay inside their tents until the wind dies down.

Winds Shape Antarctica's Surface

Blizzards also occur frequently in Antarctica. Sometimes they are so strong, they create what is called a "white-out." This means that there is so much snow in the air, you cannot see around you. Both the winds and these blizzards make Antarctica a **forbidding** place to visit.

All these different winds have a great effect on Antarctica's lands and coasts. When the strong winds move across the continent, they scrape, grate, and sculpt the icy surface. The shape of the surface is always changing and is never flat. The combination of strong winds and snowfall forms ridges of snow and ice. These ridges are called sastrugis, and they look like ice bumps or waves of snow.

19

The Shape of Snow

When you look out at Antarctica's surface, you can see miles of sastrugis. They are everywhere, and they seem to go on for miles and miles. They can be any size too. Sastrugis can be a few centimeters high. They can also be up to three meters high. It is impossible to avoid them. If you wanted to walk across Antarctica—which would be very dangerous—you would find it difficult! You might be walking on a flat surface. Then, all of a sudden, the ground might drop two or three feet.

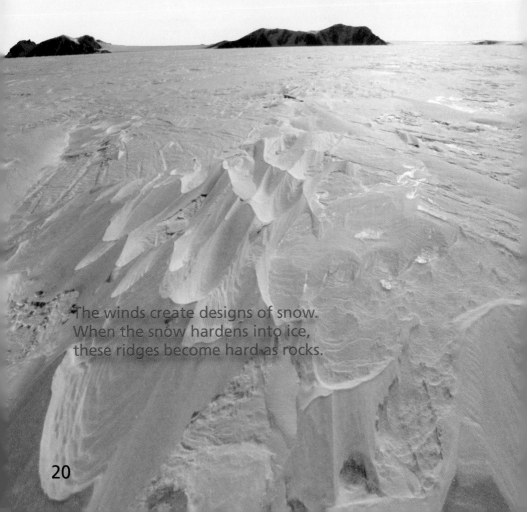

The winds create designs of snow. When the snow hardens into ice, these ridges become hard as rocks.

Wind, Salt, and Waves

Powerful winds also affect the coasts of Antarctica. They are so strong that they can push away the sea ice, exposing new areas of water to the air. The winds cool the open areas and, gradually, new ice forms.

Ocean water has a lot of salt in it. When new ice forms, a lot of salt is left behind. This makes the water below the ice of Antarctica the saltiest and densest on Earth.

With no other lands nearby to stop them, the rough Antarctic winds circle the continent, creating huge waves. The waters around the continent are known to be some of the roughest seas on Earth. It is definitely not a place for people who get seasick easily.

Ships often have a hard time in the rough seas around Antarctica.

Strong winds scrape, grate, and sculpt Antarctica's surface to form interesting designs. The icy surface is always changing.

EFFECTS OF WIND

Winds push sea ice away from Antarctica's coasts. New sea ice is formed in the open area. As the ice forms, salt is left behind in the waters. These waters are the saltiest of all the oceans.

Fierce winds create huge waves in the seas. The ocean around Antarctica is one of the roughest seas on Earth.

How Does Nature Change the Surface of the Earth?

In Antarctica, scientists study how extreme conditions affect the continent's surface. They study the effects of extreme wind, water, and ultraviolet light. Their findings help us understand how the same factors affect other parts of the Earth.

You don't need to be a scientist to see how wind, water, and light affect the Earth's surface. Look right in your own backyard! Winds can blow down trees, or rains can overflow lakes and rivers. Changes can happen over a long period of time, or they can happen all of a sudden.

At the beach, you may notice that water from the ocean washes away the sand. Beaches can erode over time. Soil can also erode. Wind can blow it away, and water can wash it away. Winds beating against hills and mountains can make rocks smooth as glass over time.

Weather can greatly change the Earth's surface in a very short period of time. Think how damaging hurricanes, tornadoes, and earthquakes can be. They can destroy everything in their paths. Rains can mix with soil to create mudslides. Earthquakes can create deep cracks in the ground. These natural changes to the Earth's surface can happen in Antarctica or anywhere else in the world.

Glossary

anticipation *n.* act of looking forward to; expectation

continent *n.* one of the seven main land masses of the Earth, including Africa, Antarctica, Asia, Australia, Europe, North America, and South America

convergence *n.* the act of coming together

depart *v.* to go away or leave

forbidding *adj.* harshly uninviting

heaves *v.* throws itself

icebergs *n.* massive floating bodies of ice broken away from an outlet glacier, ice shelf, or ice stream

Reader Response

1. State one main idea from this book. Give one or two details that support this main idea.

2. You read about the extreme conditions of Antactica. Complete the chart below.

Cause	Effect
1a.) Very cold temperatures	1b.)
2a.)	2b.) Sastrugis form
3a.) Gravity pulls cold air to the ground	3b.)

3. Some words in this book have Greek or Latin roots. For example, the word *geography* comes from the Greek words *geo* (earth) and *graphy* (to write or carve). Look up the following words in a dictionary, and write their definitions: *annually, migrate, aquatic.* See if you can find the roots of these words.

4. Look at page 23. What are some different ways to describe how winds change the Earth's surface?

Science

Genre	Comprehension Skills and Strategy	Text Features
Expository nonfiction	• Main Idea and Details • Generalize • Text Structure	• Charts • Diagrams • Heads • Maps

Scott Foresman Reading Street 4.5.4

PEARSON
Scott
Foresman

scottforesman.com

ISBN 0-328-13482-1

90000

9 780328 134823

All Things in Balance

by Tamara Jasmine Burrell

Question of the Week
What unexpected effects can humans have on nature?

High Frequency Words

nature   both
important   stop
plants   top

Concept Words

balance of nature   food chain
herbivores   omnivore
carnivores   endangered

Learning Goals

• People can upset the balance of nature.
• Plants and animals are in a food chain.
• Some animals are herbivores, and others are carnivores.